How to Draw
for
All Seasons

Barbara Soloff Levy

Dover Publications, Inc.
Mineola, New York

NOTE

Winter doesn't mean snow for everyone, but everyone knows what a snowman looks like! The springtime brings birds singing and flowers growing, and the summer is full of outdoor fun. When fall arrives, trees begin to lose their leaves, and everyone gets excited about Halloween. No matter where you live, you can always tell when the seasons are changing: the days get shorter or longer, the air gets cooler or warmer, and even the clothes you wear are different.

This entertaining and instructive book has thirty step-by-step drawings about the four seasons of the year—winter, spring, summer, and fall. Using simple shapes and lines, you will learn how to make all thirty of these drawings. Each one has several steps. Start with the simplest step (number 1). Then follow the next steps in number order. It's a good idea to trace the steps first, just to get a feel for drawing. You may want to make some changes to your pictures along the way, so it's a good idea to use a pencil. Erase the dotted lines when you get to the last step.

When you are pleased with your drawing, you can go over the lines with a felt-tip pen or a colored pencil. Finally, enjoy coloring in your picture any way you wish. After you have finished, you can think of some more ideas for drawing the seasons. Look around you. What time of year is it? Winter, spring, summer, or fall, you will find many exciting things to draw. Have fun!

Bibliographical Note

How to Draw for All Seasons is a new work, first published by Dover Publications, Inc., in 2007.

International Standard Book Number:
ISBN-13: 978-0-486-46219-6
ISBN-10: 0-486-46219-6

Manufactured in the United States of America
Dover Publications, Inc., 31 East 2nd Street, Mineola, N.Y. 11501

1

2

3

4

Snowman (Winter)   1

4   Ice Skating (Winter)

1

2

3

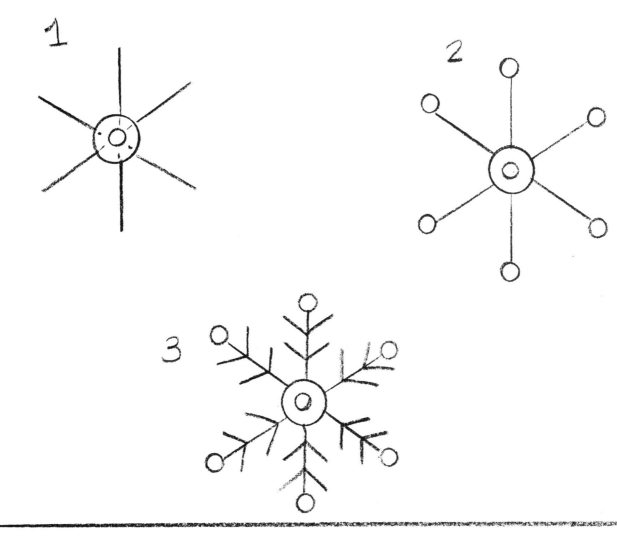

1

2

3

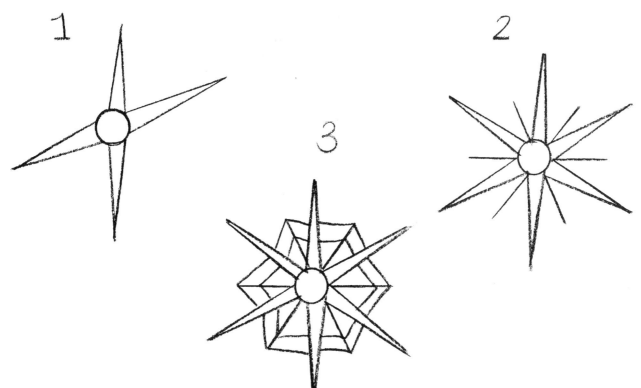

6   Hat, Scarf, Boots, and Coat (Winter)

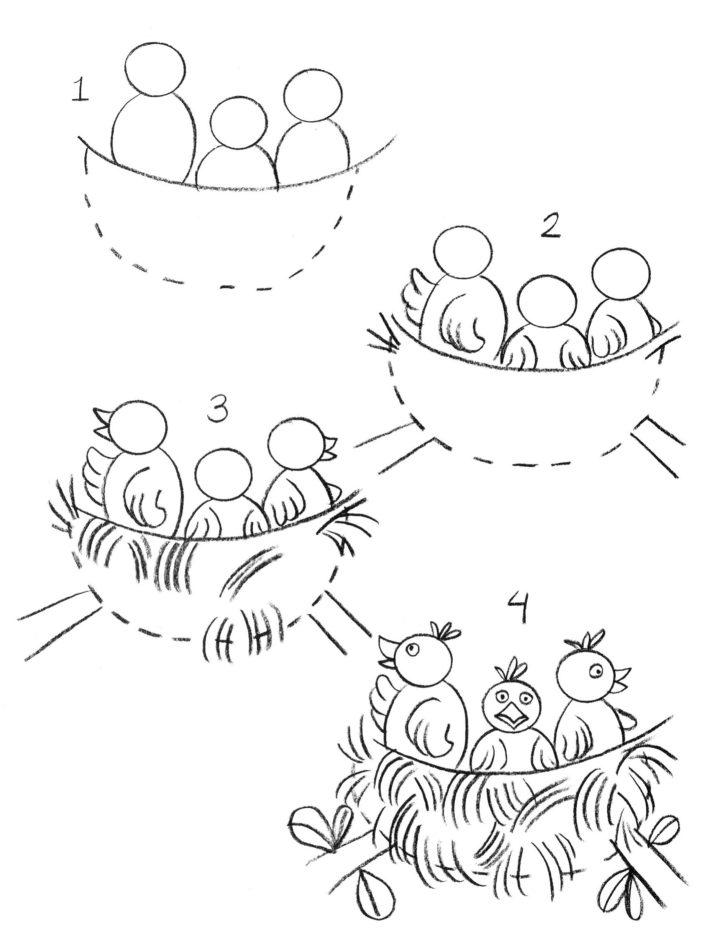

Playground Swing Set (Spring)   9

1

2

3

4

10   Playground Slide (Spring)

1

2

3

4

Flying a Kite (Spring)   11

April Showers (Spring)

Baseball Player (Spring)   13

1

2

3

4

5

6

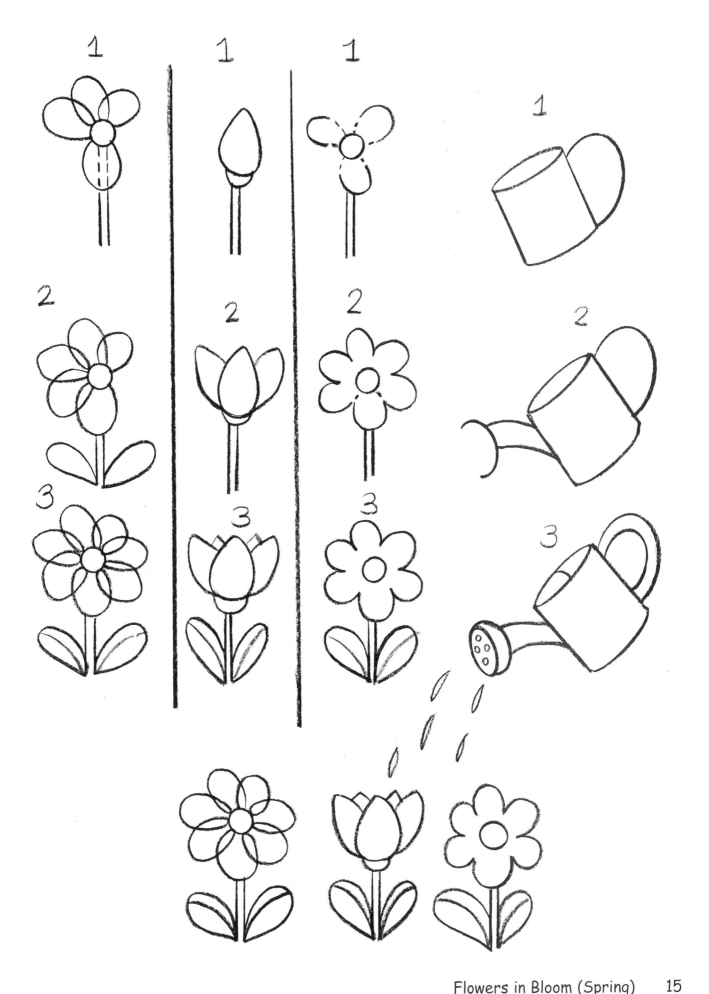

1

2

3

4

16   Flower and Bee (Summer)

1

2

Watermelon

1

2

3

Strawberry

1

2

Peach

Beach Toys and Sandcastle (Summer)

Lemonade Stand (Summer)   19

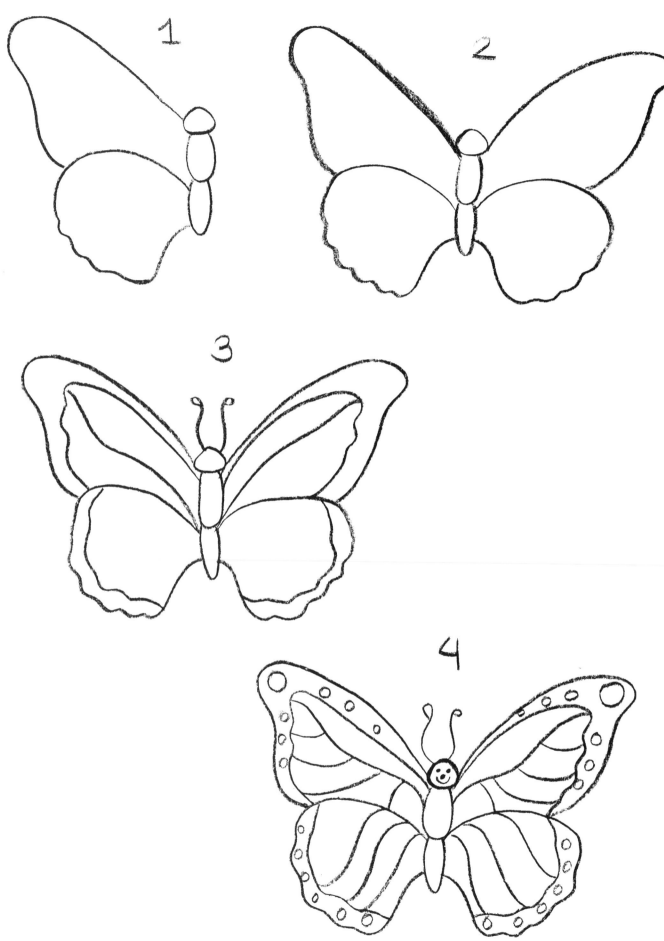

1

2

3

4

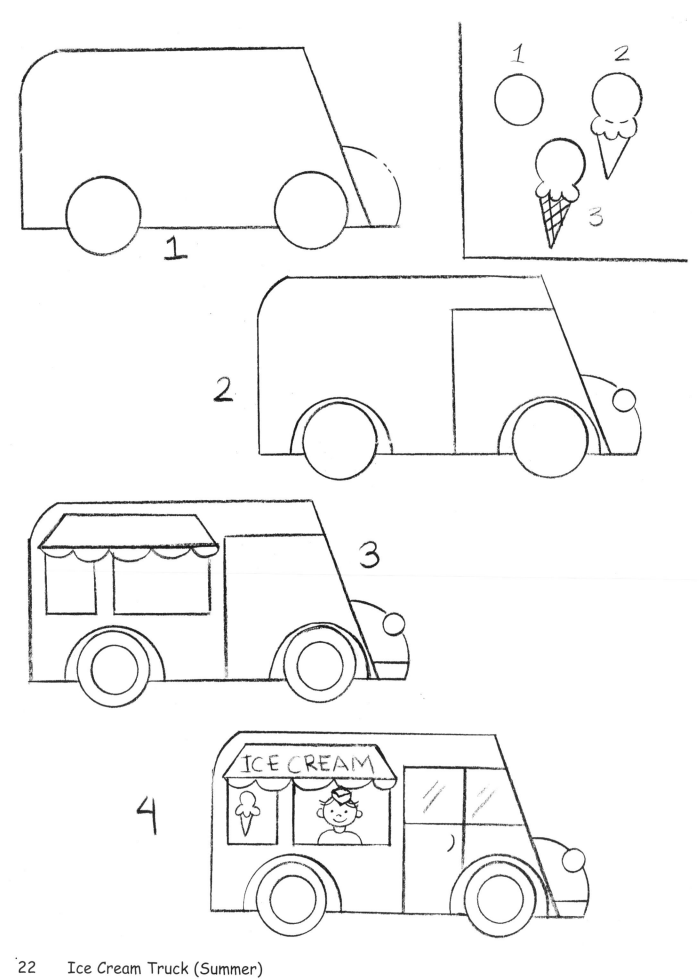

1

1 2
3

2

3

ICE CREAM

4

Diving and Swimming (Summer)   23

24   Squirrel with Acorns (Fall)

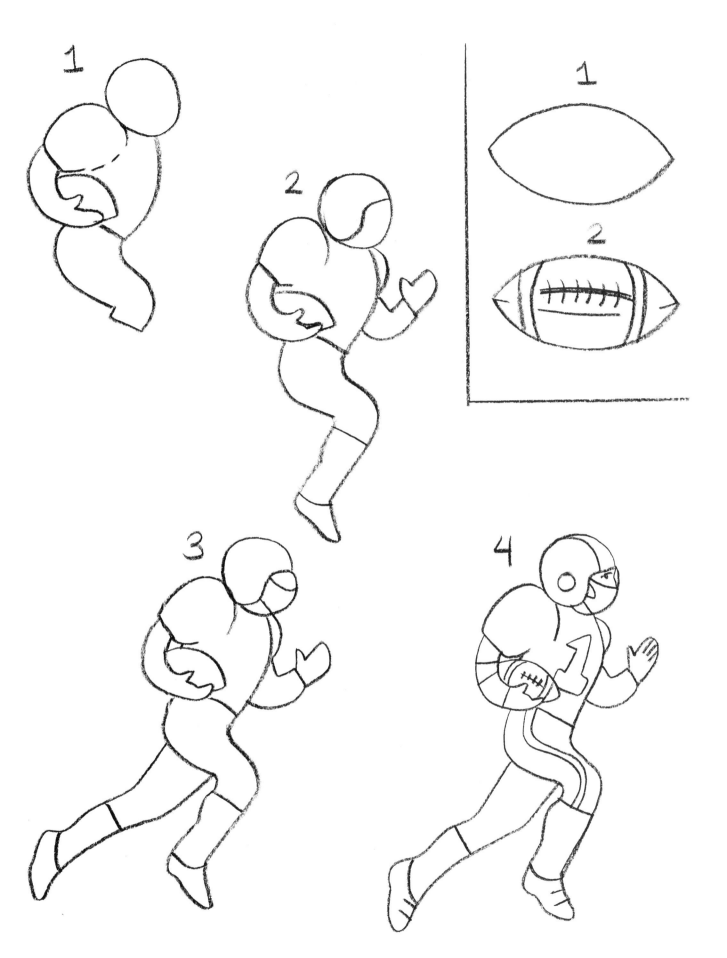

Football Player (Fall)   25

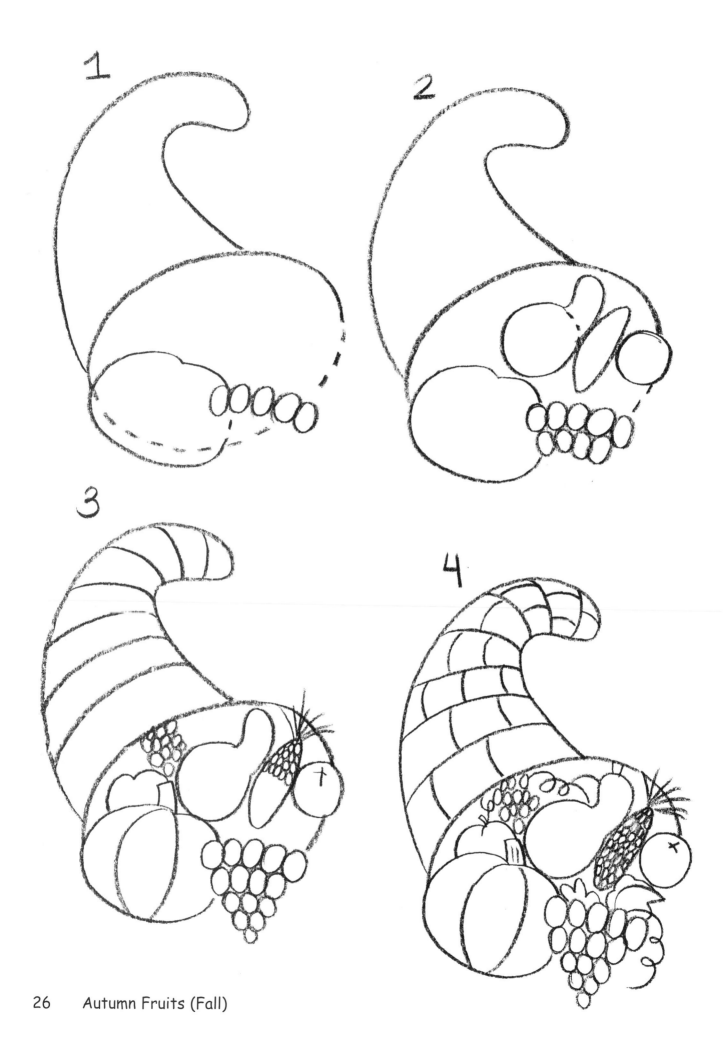

1

2

3

4

Autumn Fruits (Fall)

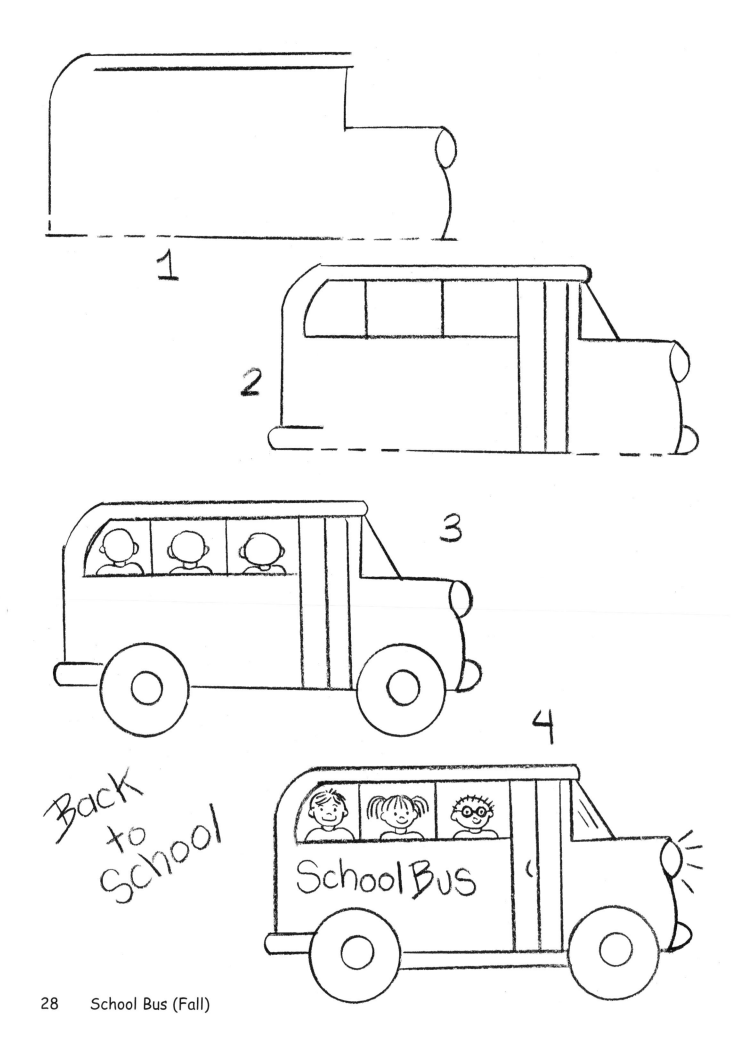

1

2

3

Back to School

4

School Bus

1

2

3

4

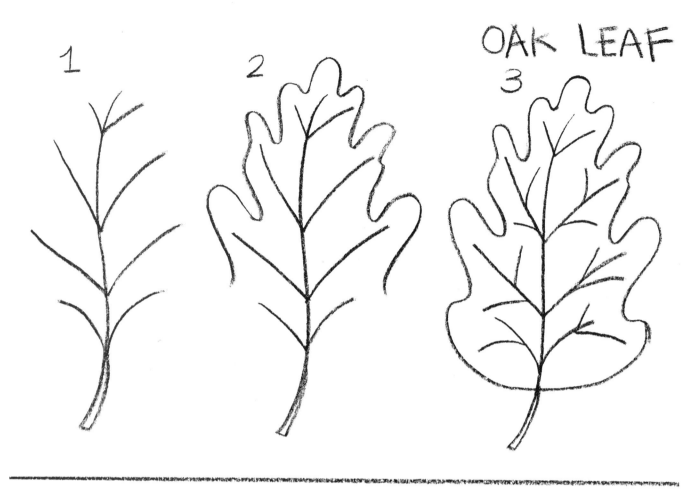

OAK LEAF

1
2
3

1
2
3

MAPLE LEAF

30   Autumn Leaves (Fall)